Created by Evgeniya Popova and Lilu Rami
Illustrations by Margarita Kukhtina

LOOK & FIND

Our Animal Friends

CLEVER
· Publishing ·

Find
the pink poodles!

Find
the smallest
dog.

Which raccoon is eating a snack?

How many raccoons are carrying masks?

Find all the sleeping raccoons.

Find seven small frogs.

Find the sleeping crocodiles.

Can you find the bird cleaning a crocodile's teeth?

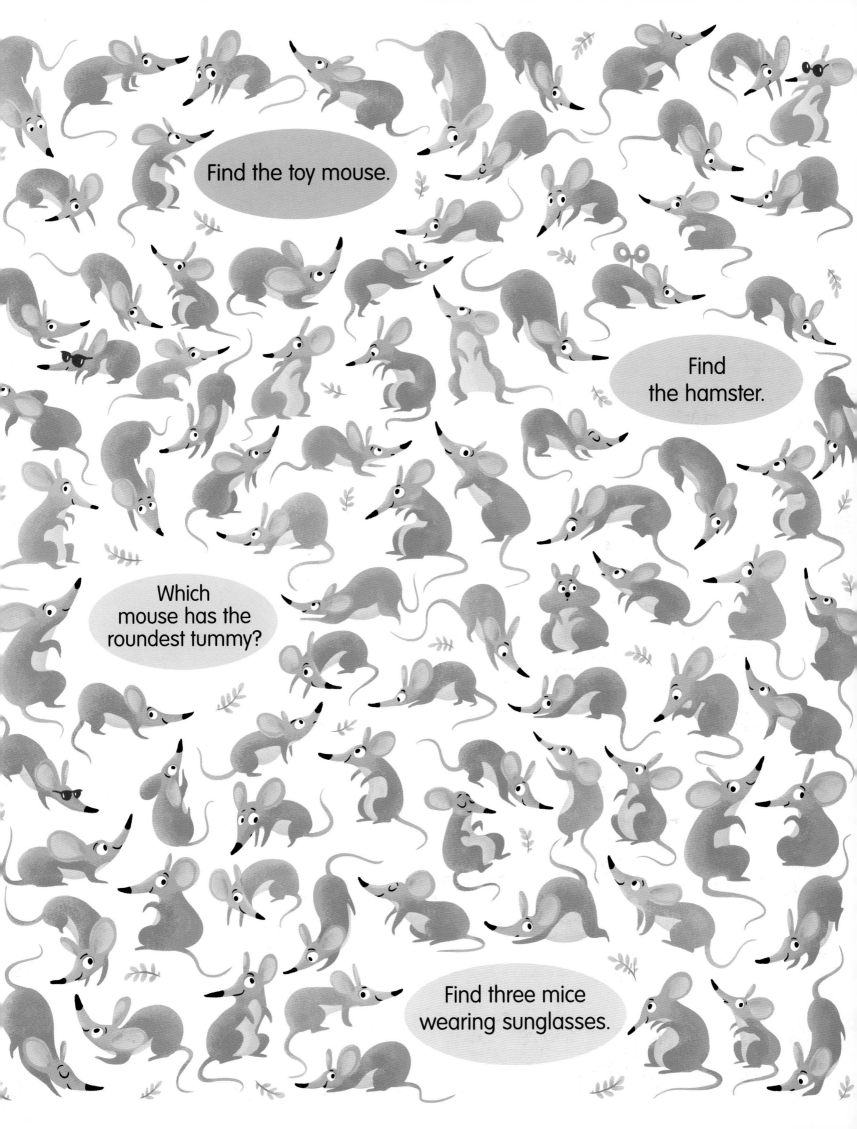

Find all
of the dragonflies.

Find
the yellow
butterflies.

Count
all the pink
butterflies.

Find the bunny with the longest ears.

Find the bunny holding a paint brush.

How many bunnies are taking a nap?

Find the littlest horses.

Find three horses with gray spots.

How many horses are wearing saddles?